100 Appliance Maintenance Tips

That Will Save You

<u>Hundreds Of Dollars</u>

Over The Life Of Your Appliances

By Mark Kochanowsky

Contents

Table Of Contents

Introduction

You may be asking yourself why a guy who makes his living repairing appliances would write a book with tips for you, the consumer, to keep your appliances working. I've worked for more than 25 years servicing and repairing appliances. My best customers are the ones who are like me and want to keep learning and save money.

Think about it! A typical, modern household can have more than 100 appliances! Don't believe me? Walk into your kitchen and take an inventory. Check out your laundry room too. Explore all your household spaces. Appliances to make our lives convenient are everywhere. We can take them for granted most of the time – until they stop working! That's where I come in with A to Z Appliance Repair. I assess what can be fixed, repair and maintain your appliances to bring out the longest value for your money.

Oh wait; let's talk about money too. Consider that your third largest expense, after your home and car, are all your appliances. Caring for these appliances by knowing the facts, getting some expert advice and following some simple practices is easier than you can imagine.

That's why I wrote this book! We should work together to keep your appliance well maintained. Being a valuable partner with my customers is the best way I know to keep them! Offering advice is part of the service I provide you while I'm caring for your appliances.

I became enthusiastic, about learning ways to maintain appliances. Along with 25 years servicing and repairing them for you. It would be fair to say that I know many ways to maintain appliances. This book focuses on the most frequent issues I've encountered in appliance repair. This is not a complete reference guide to everything you can do to maintain them.

Need more information? Let's stay in touch. Check out our A to Z Appliance Repair website (www.atozappliancerepair.net).

Now, let's get on to learning together about how to keep your appliances in great condition, so you can forget they are even in the room with you.

Mark Kochanowsky

Refrigeration Maintenance

- Once a month remove the grill off the front bottom of the refrigerator and vacuum with a narrow attachment on your vacuum hose.

- Once a year pull out the refrigerator and remove the piece of cardboard or sheet of metal at the bottom back side of the refrigerator. Then vacuum the area with a narrow attachment on your vacuum hose.

- Once a year when you pull out the refrigerator to vacuum the back also check the water line. Plastic lines dry rot after time and Copper lines build up corrosion which will cause a leak.

- During the summer months it is humid. Every time you open the freezer door a little bit of humidity makes the ice cubes stick to each other. Once a month remove the ice from the ice bucket and leave the ice bucket on the counter overnight. This way the ice will not stick to each other and dispense a lot better.

- If you have a dispenser that dispenses crushed ice and you use it, check the area that the crushed ice dispenses through on the inside of the door way. After a while this area will build up with crushed ice and stop the dispenser from working well.

- When hooking up the refrigerator to a water line, the best line to use is the metal braded water line. As said earlier the plastic water line dry rots and the copper water line will build up corrosion. Also do not use the saddle valve because after time the needle in the saddle valve will get clogged and cause problems. If necessary call a plumber to install a regular valve. Also have the valve installed behind the refrigerator so if the water needs to be shut off it can be done quickly.

- Putting the refrigerator in the garage can be a problem, Why? If you live in a region in which the temperatures drop below 50 degrees Fahrenheit, this is not good. Such temperatures could cause the oil in the compressor to thicken, leading to compressor failure or other issues. Also, refrigerator/freezer units often won't keep food frozen when the temperature of the garage drops below 35 degrees Fahrenheit.

- Do not put a lot of fluid containers on the doors. Every gallon weighs a little over 8 pounds, all the fluid will add up and damage the hinges quickly.

- Raise the front legs a little bit higher than the rear legs. This will help make the doors close.

- For Refrigerators with freezer drawers, grease the tracks yearly with Vaseline.

- Refrigerators with French Doors, every time you open the refrigerator door you let air inside the refrigerator box, due to having all the air inside the box when you slam one door shut the other will pop open.

- When installing a new Side by Side or French door refrigerator if you have an uneven floor or the refrigerator is put in a tight area this will cause the doors to look uneven at the top.

- At the top of most refrigerators is an opening where the cold air comes from the freezer side into the fresh food side. The air that is coming from the freezer side is close to the freezing temperature, if you leave a container with fluid inside it close to this area too long it can freeze up.

- Once a month take a damp cloth and wipe off the door gaskets so they don't build up with junk and shorten the life of the gaskets.

- A refrigerator that has features also has electronic boards. Have the refrigerator plugged into a surge protector.

- Keep a box of baking soda in your refrigerator to absorb the odor.

Maintaining your Wall Oven

- If the Heater Box or Element is under the floor do not put anything on the floor or you will block the heat from the Heater Box or Element and shorten the life of the parts.

- Pick up the Bake element and put a sheet of heavy duty aluminum foil underneath on the floor to catch the stuff falling down while baking.

- Use Oven Cleaner to Clean out oven body and oven racks instead of self-clean. When using self-clean the oven gets up to 900 degrees and runs for around 3 hours. The high temperature can damage electronics as well as the door lock and at times crack the door glass.

- Keep weight off the door or the hinges will be damaged.

- When installing an Electric Wall oven make sure to have an outlet. Don't have the oven hardwired to fuse box, fire hazard.

- Using Convection Bake is good on Meats, Vegetables, and Fish, but not good on Cakes, Pies, Muffins, and Cookies.

- When Baking more than one rack of cookies at once rotate the racks or the cookies on the bottom rack will receive more heat than the upper racks and bake faster or be burned.

- Right after you are done baking something don't wipe the oven door glass with a wet cloth. The wet cloth which is at a cooler temperature then the oven temperature can cause the glass to crack.

- When cleaning the console don't pull off the knobs and spray behind the knobs or use a wet cloth because the electric can be shorted out quickly with moisture.

- When following instruction on how to bake something using an old cook book and you are using convection bake you will be baking for about 20 minutes shorter time then cook book tells you.

- When using a temperature reader put the temperature reader along the back wall close to the temperature sensor in the oven or you will be getting the wrong temperature reading.

- Use a large enough cooking pan to avoid boil-overs.

- Do not store plastic items or other utensils in the oven as they may melt or burn if the oven is accidentally turned on with them inside.

- Using foil on the racks, may slow cooking and reduce browning.

- If the oven door is not closing all the way call for service right away. Because a lot of heat is escaping from the oven which is taking longer to cook something and the heat escaping will damage other parts which will make the repair more expensive.

- The oven door has a gasket to keep heat inside the oven. Over time, the gasket can become torn or deformed and this will allow heat to escape. Inspect gaskets to ensure they are in good condition and replace them as necessary.

- Glass and ceramic baking dishes cook food much more efficiently than metal pans. You can cook food just as quickly at a temperature 25 degrees cooler in a glass pan.

Maintaining your Gas Range

- Maintain top burners by cleaning the parts off with a wire brush not a wet sponge. The wet sponge will build up corrosion and lead to problems later.

- Clean off the grates, oven racks, and oven body with oven cleaner.

- Do not put the oven into self-clean. Instead clean the oven body with oven cleaner because using self-clean (running oven at 900 degrees for close to 3 hours) can damage parts.

- Use hot water and a paste of baking soda to clean difficult spots; rinse well with vinegar and water to remove all residue.

- Never use a commercial oven cleaner on a self-cleaning oven. These harsh cleaners can pit, burn, and eat into the porcelain surface

- Gas ranges with Propane will have yellow tip flames at burners at times due to fuel mixture.

Gas Flame Characteristics

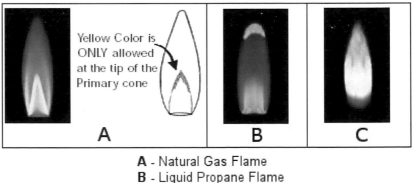

A - Natural Gas Flame
B - Liquid Propane Flame
C - **Call for Service!**

- Don't pull off the knobs and wipe with wet cloth because of the electric underneath the console will be damaged.

- Make sure the Range is on its own breaker and not plugged into a GFI outlet or an extension cord.

- When cooking with Gas versus Electric the pots will heat up much faster as well as cool down quicker.

- Do not line the broiler pan with foil, as it concentrates heat and may damage the pan.

- Do not store plastic items or other utensils in the oven as they may melt or burn if the oven is accidentally turned on with them inside.

- Using foil in the oven, especially on the racks, may slow cooking and reduce browning.

- If the oven door is not closing all the way call for service right away. Because a lot of heat is escaping from the oven which is taking longer to cook something and the heat escaping will damage other parts which will make the repair more expensive.

- Clean the inside regularly. If the inside of your oven is squeaky clean, you can be sure the heat is going into cooking your food and not the leftover pizza stuck to the bottom.

- As a range oven gets older, it is not uncommon for the oven temperature to shift. It is normal to notice some cooking time differences between a new oven and an old oven.

- You should replace the gas line if you purchase a new gas oven. Moving and swapping the ovens creates a lot of movement, and vibration which could cause leaks in the gas line. Replacing the line at this time is a small expense and a major increase in safety.

- Keep weight off door or the hinges will be damaged

- Don't cover the over floor with foil because the heater box is under the floor so you will block the heat coming from heater box.

Maintaining your Electric Range

- Keep glass top clean with glass cleaner or burn marks will be hard to remove later.

- Some burners can be pulled out. Do not pull out too many times or the socket the burner plugs into will be damaged.

- Clean off the grates, oven racks, and oven body with oven cleaner.

- Do not put the oven into self-clean. Instead clean the oven body with oven cleaner because using self-clean (running oven at 900 degrees for close to 3 hours) can damage parts.

- Never use a commercial oven cleaner on a self-cleaning oven. These harsh cleaners can pit, burn, and eat into the porcelain surface

- If the bake element is exposed then pick it up and put heavy duty foil underneath to catch the dirt.

- If the element is hidden in the floor don't cover the floor or you'll block the heat and damage the heater box.

- Clean the drip bowls after every spill or the spills with burn into the bowls and will need to be replaced

- If the oven door is not closing all the way call for service right away. Because a lot of heat is escaping from the oven which is taking longer to cook something and the heat escaping will damage other parts which will make the repair more expensive.

- Clean the inside regularly. If the inside of your oven is squeaky clean, you can be sure the heat is going into cooking your food and not the leftover pizza stuck to the bottom.

- As a range oven gets older, it is not uncommon for the oven temperature to shift. It is normal to notice some cooking time differences between a new oven and an old oven.

- Keep weight off the oven door or the hinges will be damaged.

- Don't pull off the knobs and wipe with wet sponge, electric underneath.

- When installing the range make sure to have an outlet. Do not have the range hardwired to fuse box, fire hazard.

- Right after you are done baking something don't wipe the oven door glass with a wet cloth. The wet cloth which is at a cooler temperature then the oven temperature can cause the glass to crack.

Maintaining your Gas Cook top

- Maintain top burners by cleaning the parts off with a wire brush not a wet sponge. The wet sponge will build up corrosion and lead to problems later.

- Gas Cooktops running off Propane will have yellow tip flames on burners at times due to fuel mixture.

- Don't pull off knobs and wipe with wet cloth, electric underneath the console.

- Clean off the grates with oven cleaner.

- Make sure the Cooktop is on its own breaker and not plugged into an extension cord.

- When Installing Cooktop don't put silicone around the trim or you won't be able to remove later for service.

- When using a flexible gas line to hook up to the solid pipe gas line make sure,

   a) Use maximum of one flexible gas line.
   b) Have a shut off valve installed.

Maintaining your Electric Cook top

- Keep glass top clean with glass cleaner or burn marks will be hard to remove later.

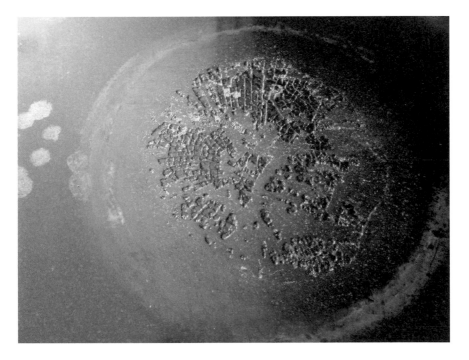

- Don't pull off the knobs and wipe with wet sponge, electric underneath.

- When Installing Cooktop don't put silicone around the trim or you won't be able to remove later for service.

- Don't use strong cleaner to keep glass top clean or the design on the glass will be worn off.

- Make sure the cooktop is on its own breaker.

- When the cook top is hot you should not place cold items or liquids on it. The thermal shock can cause the glass to crack.

- Be careful not to drop things onto the glass top (the sheet of glass is expensive.)

Maintaining Your Dishwasher

- Every other month take a bowl full of vinegar put on the top rack and run through full cycle.

- If you are single and don't use the dishwasher a lot run the dishwasher through a short cycle at least once a week.

- Clean off dishes before putting into dishwasher

- Foggy dishes indicate too much jet dry, wet dishes not enough jet dry.

- Have high loop in drain line under counter.

- Don't extend the drain line.

- Use metal braided hose for water line.

- Don't have the racks out to long while washing dishes (the weight will damage the tracks and hinges after time).

- Don't put tall object on top rack.

- If the tines are rusty sand off and use a sealant to adhere the tips over the rusty area.

- Make sure the dishwasher is on its own power line.

- Nice thin glasses and fine china silverware wash by hand.

Maintaining your Dryer

- Use time dry when drying heavy fabrics (Jeans, Towels, and Sweat Clothes).

- Use auto dry when drying light fabrics (dress up clothes).

- Clean Exhaust out yearly.

- Use 4 inch solid piping as much as possible.

- Use Plastic or Foil as little as possible, (Plastic and Foil is so dangerous that it's illegal in a lot of areas).

- Some dryer doors open up downward, don't use this type of door as a ledge to lay down clothes.

- Make sure the gas dryer is on its own breaker and don't use extension cords.

Maintaining your Front Loader Washer

- Check the pockets for items before putting into Washer. (Technicians find so many coins and other items that damage parts.)

- Leave door cracked open unless washer is running.

- Run washer through cleaning cycle every 2 months with cleaner.

- Remove the dispenser monthly and rinse under hot water.

- Check the bottom of the rubber gasket every time you empty the washer (small items like socks get stuck).

- Try not to have mixed loads (Heavy and Light fabrics) or the washer will bang around and vibrate.

- Use metal braided inlet hoses.

- Don't extend drain line

- Make sure the washer is not plugged into a GFI outlet or use extension cords.

- Make sure to have strong floor surface.

- Buy water alarm at hardware store and put on floor next to washer.

- Try not to stack dryer on top of washer. Because when time comes for service, it will be hard to do.

Maintaining Your Top Loader Washer (regular washer not water saver)

- Fill washer with dry clothes before starting washer.

- Check the pockets for items before putting into Washer, (technicians find so many coins and other items that damage parts.)

- Try not to have mixed loads (Heavy and Light fabrics)

- Use metal braided inlet hoses instead of the black rubber ones.

- Don't extend drain line

- Make sure the elbow in the drain line has no kink.

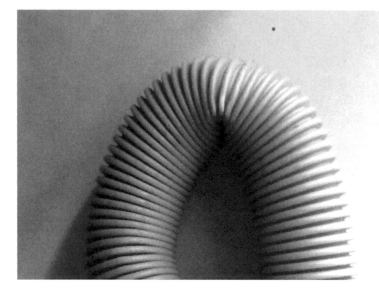

- Don't use the delicate speed cycle on a full load.

- Buy water alarm at hardware store and put on floor next to washer.

- Make sure the washer is not plugged into a GFI outlet and don't use extensions cords.

- Don't run the washer through a cycle set on cold water all the time.

Maintaining Your Electric Water Heater

- Drain the tank yearly.

- Have Tank on bricks off the floor.

- Make sure the Tank is level.

- Buy water alarm and put on the floor next to the tank.

- Check the fittings yearly for corrosion build up yearly.

Maintaining Your Gas Water Heater

- Drain the tank yearly.

- Clean the burner with a soft wire brush yearly.

- Have Tank on bricks off the floor.

- Make sure the Tank is level.

- Buy water alarm and put on the floor next to the tank.

- Check the fittings for corrosion build up yearly.

CPSIA information can be obtained at www.ICGtesting.com
Printed in the USA
LVIW01n1425110517
534159LV00006B/75